James Joyce's Water Closet

poems by

Heather Corbally Bryant

Finishing Line Press
Georgetown, Kentucky

James Joyce's Water Closet

Copyright © 2018 by Heather Corbally Bryant
ISBN 978-1-63534-786-9 First Edition
All rights reserved under International and Pan-American Copyright Conventions. No part of this book may be reproduced in any manner whatsoever without written permission from the publisher, except in the case of brief quotations embodied in critical articles and reviews.

ACKNOWLEDGMENTS

With thanks, as always, to my colleagues, my family, my friends, and my students.

Publisher: Leah Maines

Editor: Christen Kincaid

Cover Art: Abigail Katz

Author Photo: Heidi Lynne Photography,
　　　　　http://www.heidilynnephotography.com

Cover Design: Leah Huete

Printed in the USA on acid-free paper.
Order online: www.finishinglinepress.com
　　　　　also available on amazon.com

Author inquiries and mail orders:
Finishing Line Press
P. O. Box 1626
Georgetown, Kentucky 40324
U. S. A.

Table of Contents

Arriving in Ireland at Six in the Morning 1

A Sparrow 2

James Joyce's Water Closet 3

On the Train to Galway, Just Past Kildare 4

In Teach Ban, The White Cottage 5

Kingstown Bay 6

Renvyle Peninsula 7

A trip to Inishbofin, or the Island of the White Cow 8

The Lady Maureen 9

An Accident off Kingstown Bay 10

High Island 11

Grazing 12

Clifden Castle 13

Kill Cemetery 14

On Dolphin Beach 15

The Burren 16

Ballinalacken Castle 17

Lost Passports 18

For my children, who show me the way

Arriving in Ireland at Six in the Morning

The plane bumps to the ground; from above we have been peering
Out the window, patchwork of soft greens, divided into hedgerows—
Have been appearing below, now they stretch out to the side, these

Fields of land, solid and everlasting—we stretch and gather our
Belongings, squinting even at this cloudy, showery day, a steady mist
Seeping down upon us as we depart customs, seeking a taxi through

Morning rush hour, fumes of diesel and daredevils bicyclists, darting
Across our path, having plunged ourselves into the quotidian
Routine of the countryside across the sea from us—

The particularity of the inconsequential.

A Sparrow

Years before in graduate school, I walk into the library after
Dinner and begin to conjugate Old English verbs in my head—
In my square of light, I spread out my papers and begin—

I like the order of the pages, the routine, every evening, I must
Make my way through fifty lines of translation; I start in pencil
So that I can erase my mistakes; afterwards, I will copy the lines

Onto my assignment sheet—this night, I learn of Grendel's banquet
And, in time, the twilight of winter when a small hardy sparrow flew by
To entertain the guests, surprised by its haplessness; this,

I see will not be the life for me—I will find a way into the world.

James Joyce's Water Closet

By the river Liffey, we pass a brick row of houses, yellow door swung
Halfway open as if beckoning us inside—the rooms are open, airy, and
   spare—
Empty of furniture, just musty paintings—nothing leftover of the life
   lived

There, only the creaky stairs, bumpy rails, uneven floors; we step across
The threshold and climb up to the top where my children pull the string
To flush the toilet so many times it snaps in their hands—I apologize
   and

We continue towards the dining room where we pause, walls
Maroon and green, this is the scene I recognize, the place where Joyce
Wrote his ghostly story, "The Dead," here is where his pen gave his

Characters life; as we descend I see him sitting and writing there.

On the Train to Galway, Just Past Kildare

I know that you—my children—are only passing through
Our lives—as just a moment in stop-time—as we journey
Across Ireland on this Sunday morning, having left Dublin for

The quiet of post-bacchanalian, on our way past countryside
Hedges of various shades of green, sprinkles of orange poppies,
Two women riding horses down to a stream, a speckled fawn

Calf ambling towards her mother, waiting by a barn, lonely
On their farm, as each step takes them a bit further afield, just
As you three children will grow, stepping away from us a

Little further each day; I would not wish it any other way.

In Teach Ban, The White Cottage

In my deepest sleep, dreams come to me quickly—I wake
Slowly, images still pressed against my eyelids; in the dawn, I
Know not where I am, only that I am afraid, afraid of what I

Have dreamed—along the margins I have written, rape dream
In faint letters, as though I could only whisper the truth, and
Barely even to myself—I alone possess myself—the pictures

Dissipate before I can gather them into meaning—they slip
Through my hands, night stars cut into the sky fading before I
Can catch them—I can't be held too close— a part of

Me needs to break free, to own my own body in this white house.

Kingstown Bay

We unfold the map, smoothing out the creases—the roads
Scatter, narrow, fanning out into the countryside—we pass
Through villages—Tullycross, Reless, Moycollan, and

Oughterend—the road slows through main streets—pastel
Colored shops, post offices, surgeries, pubs, a collie guarding
The hens' gate—we stop for lunch and then climb the sky

Road at Clifden until we are teetering above Mannin Bay,
Edged against the stone walls, crows and sheep grazing
Along the green grass, ghosts fields once tended by long-gone

Farmers, long gone from this land, this earth, this universe.

Renvyle Peninsula

Clouds clear, a sunburst appears where, just minutes before,
Clouds were scattering rain—the bay appears before us—
Water now cerulean blue, soft with the new light in the sky—

We are so far north, just past the solstice that twilight lasts
Forever here; at eleven o'clock we could still go for a walk and
See our footing along the path—here, we skip down over the

Bulging rocks, surprised by their depth, waves crashing
Through the granite houses—behind us, cows lumber along,
Passing a clothesline filled with clean laundry strung from

A sixteenth-century ruined keep—stone against grass and sky.

A Day at Inishbofin, or the Island of the White Cow

Checking the sky, we pack a picnic, and prepare to walk
The perimeter of this island—the ferry ride takes us past
The small spots of land ringing the shore until we squeeze

Through the narrow opening to the harbor—at the entrance,
Piles of old stone still guard the strait where Grace O'Malley
Once declared herself Pirate Queen of this green and fertile

Island—we dock, debark, and begin our journey by foot around
This round point of land, population one hundred and eighty people;
We eat lunch along the shore, hearing waves crashing above, until

We rush back to buy ice cream before the last ferry arrives.

The Lady Maureen

The day dawns dim, dismal, sheets of rain pound against our front
Windows—we wonder aloud if the fishing is still on; an elderly man
Knocks on our door and tells us to meet him at the harbor in less than
Half an hour—we prepare a picnic and are off again—walking down
The lane; rain pelts beating down upon us—we climb aboard the rattling
Boat and head off shore—a party of seven, leaving Kingstown Harbor—
Jan, we learn is the captain's name, he speaks mostly in Swedish, but
Tells the kids to look for the fishies—and we begin, just past High
    Island—
The rods go on—you my youngest, catch the first pollack, and from
    there,
We're off—Jan puts his hand over my daughter's reel, and within seconds,
She has pulled in six fish on one line—we return at day's end with a haul
Of cod, mackerel, and pollock—seals watched us from their rocks—we
Jump in a dinghy and are taken ashore—in the meantime, we've downed
Warm coffee, sweetened, from tin cups, as well as soup and salt and
Vinegar crisps—we've all been jostled around a bit, but the day was
    worth
It—the kids walk up the hill to distribute most of the fish to the villagers
While we coat the keep with butter and flour to sauté in a big frying pan,
The kids delight in the idea we are eating fish caught by their own hands.

An Accident off Kingstown Bay

The fisherman pointed his finger across
The way toward an azure bay, water swirling
Clear beneath white sand—a sunny June day,
Peace serene reigns here—it would be impossible
To imagine a disaster taking place in this scene; just
Over there, he continued, a young couple came
Over from London, a girl and her boyfriend,
To attend a party at the old red schoolhouse, that
One set by the bend in the Clifden road—it got
Loud and they went out for a dip—she first, he
Following—until a rip tide caught them;
They found his body first, faraway from shore—
Long after the search had been called off, her
Remains washed in, riding the tide of the solstice.

High Island

For eight centuries, maybe more, this land has been cultivated,
Shaped, and worn, lived on and through, obdurate and pure—
On this rocky outpost of the Atlantic, monks settled first, they
Built a church out of stone, a small fortress, but mostly, they
Lived in caves set in the ledges on the edges facing the shore, a
Life of faith and difficulty, they would be very lucky even to live
Past forty—rocks often were made into tombs, uneven and spare
Where they sought shelter against the brutal wind; when they
Were able, they fished and ate berries hidden in the fields;
Everything they needed was right here, in this austere land—
Of earth, fire, water, and air—from there across the lough, it
Must have been a wretched life, but a beautiful one too—now,
When we pass by, we can sense the mysteries hidden there, held in
The age of the land, the harshness of jutting rock against dark skies.

Grazing
    For Phoebe

Each evening, when the long light lingers, you and I walk up through
The pasture—at the first, you spot two mares with their foals; you cut
Up carrots for our outing and the horses feed easily, touching our hands
With their soft mouths; sometimes they have already climbed to the top
Of the hill where the nettles are thinner and the grass still green; while
The mother eats, the foal stands by and watches; when she sees us leave,
She'll put her head against her mother's udder, give a tug, and begin to
    feed—
Just as she needs, as you fed not so very long ago from me, a world away
    in
Your terms—at night, a trailer comes to take the pair away; two boys
    round
Up the beasts with whips; you are disconsolate, you who feel things with
Such intensity—I see your sadness and long for the morning when it will
    be a
New day—and we can visit one more time—we look away, the foal
scampers around
In an unsteady circle—knowing that something is about to change utterly.

Clifden Castle

The days last so long here—by the northern lights, the Gulf Stream
Warming our climate, making fuchsia and calla lilies and stunted
Palm trees grow, toppled by the wind—we feel free, untethered

To any other routine than the light, the land, and the tides—we park
And scamper through an old gate lodge in search of yet another ruin;
This time what remains of a castle pokes up—half staircases clinging

To the pieces of a tower; the lace grows around; this place has been
Marked as too dangerous to climb so we turn to go, curiosity piqued
About what it must have been like to live here so very long ago—

The ruins are what we have left to read, what stays to the last.

Kill Cemetery

On our last afternoon, sky gray and full with rain, I set out again
For a place I have yet to find; twice before, I've been unsuccessful;
Once, I turned the wrong way and went too far, meeting up with
The main road before finding my left; a salty man waylaid me and
Explained to me what I might find there; he lay down in the grass,
And wanted me to as well; instead, I stood while he told me talk
Of long ago when the archeologists came to the place and he hid
The grave, and misled the experts about the location of the bog
People—no sense in getting the know-it-alls involved anytime
Soon; they would just make a mess of things, nothing more; but, if
I looked past the last graves, there I would see the mound, hidden
Under the burrs by the part that has not been mowed in years;

In Ireland, nothing gets in the way of the story, not one thing; in
Between splashes of wetness, my feet soaked from the wet grass
Soaked with dew, I fork left, then left again; two white pups
Follow me for a short while, until they become distracted by
Another passerby—I lift one gate over the stones, untie the bow
Knot at the next one, the iron which keeps the cows, horses, and
Sheep out—here, all is simplicity—long grass, tall stones, wedged
Against the winds; the head markers face towards the water so as
To get the best view over the land, to the hills beyond; whole
Families are buried here, and young, too—by the dates, it looks
As though you're doing well if you get past thirty—infants too, and
A young boy as well as a young girl, a son and a daughter together,
No mention of a mother—a few black flies buzz around me—

I tour the perimeter, having put the camera away—it doesn't seem
Right to photograph the dead—besides, I have just read an article
That says, once we photograph something we cease to remember it;
Here, I notice the artificial flowers, blue, green, yellow, and pink—
Too bright to be real, set against wedges of stone, rectangles dug
Into the earth; some graves homemade, stucco decorated with
Seashells, for those lost at sea; I close the gate behind me—and
Walk back to the cottage, watching for rain from the darkening sky.

On Dolphin Beach

Just down the way, the wavy road forks and winds until
It branches off into three—beach way, sky way, or the road
To town—we choose the one leading towards Dolphin Beach,

Down a rutted, stony track, with barely space enough for one
Car's width—at the end, we came to the last of the land, looking
West at sunset over the Atlantic Ocean, the last piece of earth

Until Brooklyn, the shortest distance across the sea, crossing
With the crows; it's a miniature world here, a world with
Minnows, snails, mollusks, oysters, maybe a puffin or two—

A pair of dogs chase rocks into the water; my children play
With the rounded stones, smoothed out of Connemara marble,
White now in my hand—we build barriers and tunnels in

Softening sand until water laps across our toes and it's time to go.

The Burren

Everything seems flipped in this country—you cannot get there
From here; the roads are narrow, we drive on the wrong side, as
If life is lived in reverse—the skies open with rain, even though we

Can see sunshine across the way; the Cliffs of Moher are not marked
On our map; stores are closing, and we cannot find a place wide enough
By the side of the road to park—in these layers of limestone grooved

With heather, we might as well be on the moon—we wouldn't get
There until almost dark, we might as well have driven in a circle—
Clumps of rock and wild flower—my son takes a small walk to see what

He can—we think we are lost until a sign for our hotel rises out of the
    mist.

Ballinalacken Castle

Out of the mist that rains, passing in clumps in front of us, we see a castle
Waiting—we might as well be in the nineteenth century looking for a
   hostelry
To shelter us from a storm—we turn in through the gates, round the wide,

Grassy curve until we see a stone tower, a ruin from another era, a fortress
To guard this point above the cliffs, we rush through spots of rain until we
Enter the warmth of a peat fire; I toss our sodden clothes in a dryer—
   when

We sit down to dinner, the sky clears, patches of blue sky appear and
Later we see the Aran islands, and a vivid rendition of "Wish
You Were Here," plays in the background—we sip whiskey and glimpse

The lights from Inishmere—you are never very far from water here.

Lost Passports

Life can so easily be lived backwards—on the morning we are due
To fly out of Shannon, our passports are nowhere to be found—now
It is easy to see how we lost them—we who could rarely talk about

Anything—it is easy to see how we left them in a drawer in our Dublin
Hotel and didn't think about them again until a few hours before
    departure—
Through the kindness of strangers, we made our way home amidst the

Comfort and tutters of "Oh, Americans do this all the time—" it was a
    miracle,
Really, that they let us go without them—one scenario involved a taxi
    driving
Them across Ireland on a Sunday—but in the end, as long as we had

The numbers they let us leave—a small sign that we could not stay.

Heather Corbally Bryant (formerly Heather Bryant Jordan) teaches in the Writing Program at Wellesley College. Previously, she taught at the Pennsylvania State University, the University of Michigan, and Harvard College where she won awards for her teaching. She received her A.B. with honors in History and Literature from Harvard where she received the Boston Ruskin Prize for her thesis. She received her PhD in Modern British and Irish Literature from the University of Michigan where she was a Regents Fellow.

Her academic publications include, *How Will the Heart Endure: Elizabeth Bowen and the Landscape of War* (University of Michigan Press, 1992) which received the Donald Murphy Prize for best first book. She has also assisted in the research for the Cornell Yeats Series as well as publishing academic articles in *Review, Text, The New Hibernia Review,* and *The Library Chronicle of the University of Texas at Austin,* among others. She has given papers at international conferences and was a plenary speaker at the centennial celebration of Elizabeth Bowen held at University College, Cork.

Beyond her academic publications, Heather Corbally Bryant has published a work of creative nonfiction, *You Can't Wrap Fire in Paper* (Ardent Writer Press, 2018) as well as seven books poetry: *Cheap Grace* (The Finishing Line Press, 2011), *Lottery Ticket* (The Parallel Press Series of the University of Wisconsin at Madison, 2013), *Compass Rose* (The Finishing Line Press, 2015), *My Wedding Dress* (The Finishing Line Press, 2016), *Thunderstorm* (The Finishing Line Press, 2017), and *Eve's Lament* (The Finishing Line Press, 2018). *Island Dream Songs,* her eighth collection, is forthcoming in 2019 from The Finishing Line Press. She has also published poems in *The Christian Science Monitor, In Other Words, Fourth & Sycamore,* and

The Old Frog Pond Farm Chapbooks. James Joyce's Water Closet, her seventh book of poems, won honorable mention in The Finishing Line Press Open Chapbook Competition. *Thunderstorm* was nominated for a 2018 Massachusetts Book Award, and her poem, "The Easterly," has just been nominated for a Pushcart Prize. She has given readings at universities, conferences, and bookstores across the United States and in Ireland.

Heathercorballybryant.com

www.ingramcontent.com/pod-product-compliance
Lightning Source LLC
LaVergne TN
LVHW041523070426
835507LV00012B/1791